The Roadmap to Common Sense Investing

Detailed approach to personal growth,
money management, and investing

© Maxim Soleno, Engineer
All right reserved.
No part of this book may be reproduced.

ISBN-13: 979-8-6870-8116-0

Disclaimer:

Please note that the author is not a financial nor an investment advisor and does not advise on which securities individuals should invest in. The author will not assume any responsibility or undertake any liabilities for investment results.

The examples provided in this book are for educational purposes only and readers should do their own research and due diligence when making any sort of investment decisions. There are always different degrees of risks and uncertainties involved when it comes to investing so it is crucial that you understand those risks before making decisions which should not solely be based on information obtained from this book. In addition, it should not be assumed that following the examples in this book will lead to profitability. When it comes to finance, it is highly recommended that you speak with a licensed financial advisor who can help you create a plan to reach your goals.

Table of Contents

Introduction

Chapter 1: Invest in yourself

Chapter 2: Pay Down Debt

Chapter 3: Emergency Fund

Chapter 4: Investing in the Stock Market

Chapter 5: Streams of Income

Chapter 6: Cash is Trash

Chapter 7: Diversification

Chapter 8: Stay Focused

Final Words

Glossary

INTRODUCTION

This book is intended to help you get started with investing in all areas of your life and will serve as a guide for you to set the correct expectations. We will cover some of the fundamentals along with real life examples to help you get equipped with the skills you need to achieve your goals. You will also get an understanding of what it is you need to focus on, why, and how to get started with personal development and financial management. My recommendation is not to skip any chapters as I have organized them in the order of importance and priority. Now, sit back and enjoy the ride.

This book is all about common sense investing so it shouldn't come as a shock when I say: the greatest asset in your life is YOU. First and foremost, you need to focus on you. You have to evaluate your strengths and weaknesses. You need to focus on your happiness and well-being. If you are not happy, that's where the majority of your efforts should be invested in. At the end of the day, money should just be a means to reduce your stress and make you happier in life; not the other way around.

In chapter 2, we concentrate on the importance of paying down your debts. It is crucial to be cautious of debt as it can have a dangerous domino effect in your life if you don't get a good handle on it. There is absolutely no good reason to invest your money and income in other areas until you have gotten rid of your short-term debt at the least and have built up a solid emergency fund to provide you support in time of need.

Next, we discuss investing in the stock market which has a very broad spectrum. As you will soon see, there is a certain level of risk associated with investing in the market. It is imperative that you require the knowledge necessary to de-risk your portfolio using diversification through vehicles such as fixed-income assets. Anybody can buy and sell stocks these days. Understanding your risk level and balancing that risk with the correct asset allocation is what will set you aside from everyone else who loses money in the market.

Chapter 5 focuses on having multiple sources of income streams. Most successful people have at least more than one source of income. In fact, an average millionaire has approx. 7 income streams. Having multiple sources of income can help provide a certain level of freedom and to help you reach your goals sooner than anticipated. Multiple sources of income will increase your overall cash flow which in turn can help you with unemployment, paying down debt, rising cost of living, and paying for those dream vacations.

When it comes down to investing in yourself and your life, success never comes easy and certainly not without trade-offs. You have to be motivated, driven, and maintain a high level of consistency. Believe in yourself and make your dreams come true.

This book will provide the proper guidelines for you

to build a foundation on financial literacy and gain the proper money management skills required to become more self-sufficient. This should help you reach your goals and prevent you from making poor financial decisions.

I have included a glossary at the end of this book for your convenience. If you come across words that you don't understand, please refer to the definitions in the glossary at the back of this book.

CHAPTER 1: INVEST IN YOURSELF

Oftentimes when most people want to start investing or just starting to get familiar with the concept, they immediately jump into things such as the stock market, real estate, minerals(such as gold), investing in other businesses(such as startups), and so on. One of the issues with these types of investments is the need for initial capital or the "seed money" if you will. Another problem is the level of education required to be able to make such investment decisions. But the biggest issue, in my opinion, is the priority of this type of investment.

As you may have already heard this saying, the best investment you can make is in yourself and for a good reason. I mean think about it: your body and your mind are the two assets you need to carry yourself through this life and overcome the challenges it will put on your path. And needless to say, before being able to invest in yourself effectively, you need to know yourself or begin to learn. Try and begin evaluating yourself by asking these questions:
- Are you happy?
- Are you where you're supposed to be at this stage in

your life?
- Do you maintain a good physical and mental state?
- Are you happy with your career and growth?
- Do you have short-term and long-term plans in life?
- Are you well-off financially or are you struggling?

These are just a few questions you can ask yourself to get a better sense of where you are at the moment. Notice that I purposely put the "money question" as the last point in the list because it represents the least importance at this stage. What good is money when you are not happy or if you don't have your health?

Whether you are happy or not, it is very crucial to understand why you are making the decisions you are and how the consequences affect your life. Once you are able to identify the reasons behind your decisions, you can learn from them and adjust accordingly to continue towards the path of happiness. This is one of the best investments you can make in your entire life. When you are happy everything else naturally falls into place.

Maintaining a good physical and mental state is just as equally important. If you are stressed, you need to take the time to identify the reasons behind it. Is your stress related to work or your career? Are you having issues with friends or family members? Are you having problems with debt? Regardless of the reason, you need to prioritize your emotional well being. Meditation has been proven to help reduce stress and has worked for the majority of people so be sure to give that a try. There are several different types of meditation (guided vs non-guided for example) and only you will be able to tell which one works best for you. There are also a lot of different free(and paid) meditation apps out there that you can download and use on your mobile phone which will help you get started. Everyone has some downtime throughout the day so if you are commuting to and from work via metro/transit or have 5-10 min during lunch time, be sure to give this a try. One thing I would personally recommend is to learn and practice different breathing and relaxation techniques which helps increase self-awareness. There are a lot of different tutorials out there on the internet that you can refer to as reference.

Exercising and eating healthy is essential in maintaining a healthy lifestyle. People who exercise often tend to have lower heart rates which in turn can help with having a good night sleep. Lack of sleep can put a lot of stress on your body and may affect you in ways you might not be aware of. Stretching exercises such as Yoga can help maintain a good blood flow throughout your body and muscles and helps reduce stress. Eating healthy will ensure your body is getting enough vitamins and antioxidants naturally(without taking off-the-counter supplements) helping improve your cardiovascular health.

One thing I can't emphasize enough: consistency is key. Just because you practiced meditation for 10 minutes last night, it won't mean you will be less stressed today. Just because you went to the gym and worked out 5 out of 7 days last week, it doesn't mean you will lose the weight you were hoping for. It takes weeks or months of deduction and consistency before seeing any results. So don't give up if you try something and you don't see immediate results. Stay motivated and inspired. If you are trying something for a long time and you are not seeing results, then you are most likely doing it wrong. Invest in some time and research to see what mistakes you are making so that you can learn from them and improve. Life is simply a collection of trial and error experiments.

On a final note, if you think you have put in the time and have tried everything and are still not getting any results, then consider talking to a professional and seek help. There are people who have specific education and dedicate their careers in the mentioned above fields. They deal with many different cases and scenarios and chances are they will be able to help you whether it's physical or emotional. Many employers these days offer health benefits which might include a set allocated dollar amount for psychology, dietitian, or even a gym membership so be sure to take advantage of those if you are in need of help.

If you are a working professional, you can probably guess that we spend almost half of our lives at our workplace. Some of us even spend more time at work than we do with our partners or kids. So it is very crucial and almost a necessity to be happy about the type of work you do and your passion for it considering an average individual spends roughly 30-40 years of their life in the workforce. In addition, it is very important that you get compensated well for your services and time so that you can maintain a good and happy lifestyle.

If you are working at a job that you don't enjoy, then consider investing your time and money in getting the education that will help you towards getting a job you are passionate about.
I would like to walk you through a real life example but please keep in mind the numbers mentioned below might differ based on country, region, or even per employer:
Let's say you work as a support analyst at an IT company making $40k/year and you don't quite enjoy what you

do. You don't like answering phone calls and dealing with frustrated and angry customers (don't get me wrong some people like doing this). However, you have always had a passion for coding and you even have side projects that you work on during your own leisure time.

Let's say you have $1000 that you would like to invest. One of your immediate thoughts might be to invest this money into the stock market. Yes, historically the stock market has made many people rich but let's crunch through some numbers:

The U.S. stock market (S&P 500) has historically generated roughly about ~7-10% return per year since inception. If you were to invest your money in an S&P 500 Index Fund(we will cover this in later chapters), at best, you will get a 10% return according to historical stats. This means your $1000 is now worth $1100 after 1 year.

Now let's pretend you don't invest this money in the stock market and instead you invest this money in yourself. You sign up for some online courses related to programming, or take a course at a local college/university, or sign up for a 3-month coding bootcamp. Once you acquire the necessary skill set, you start applying for development jobs and you get hired as a junior software developer making $55k/year. You are now making $15k more per year moving forward.

You tell me, which one is a better investment? In the first option, you increased your $1000 by $100 in one year. In the second option, you used the $1000 on self development and you increased your salary by $15000. That is $15000 more you are making every year which you could use to also invest in the stock market. But more importantly, if you took the second option, not only you have increased your financial net worth, but you are also working at a job that you enjoy and are passionate about.

I myself work in the technology sector and I work with people who have gone through this process and it has changed their lives for the better. I can see that they have a greater sense of appreciation and self satisfaction doing what they do today than what they did or studied before. Not to mention a lot more money which now they can use to invest in other areas of life and diversify. Although the above example highlights the technology sector, the idea is the same across all industries.

Always invest in yourself by advancing your education and developing new skill sets which will help propel you into a fulfilling and promising career you will enjoy.

And I will leave you with this: "An investment in knowledge pays the best interest." - **Benjamin Franklin**

CHAPTER 2: PAY DOWN DEBT

Paying down debt is often a tricky topic for people to wrap their heads around. This is simply because everyone thinks of debt as the money they need to pay back over a period of time which is correct to some extent. This makes paying down debt less attractive from an investment point of view. Naturally as human beings, we would prefer to spend or invest our hard earned cash in anything else. But what if we look at debt from a different perspective? Consider the following: the money you don't have to pay, is the money you make.

When you begin to collect debt, you are digging yourself into a hole that will be more difficult to come out of over time so the best first thing to do is to try avoiding debts all together. But life doesn't always work out the way we want it to so we need to be realistic. If you take out a loan from the bank for a business, you will have to repay that loan back over time. If you make purchases using your credit card, you will need to pay the balance. If you are taking out a student loan to attend college or university, you have to pay that money back over time after graduation. If you take on a mortgage to buy a house, you need to pay that back.

YOU SIMPLY JUST HAVE TO. If you don't, banks and creditors can destroy your credit and seize your assets which will make your life a lot more difficult in the future. And our goal is to make life easier, not harder.

Now that we have established the fact that "you have to pay down your debt" periodically and understanding that debts and loans are usually associated with a certain interest rate, let's walk through a simple example.

Let's say you take out a $50,000 student loan to attend post secondary education and obtain a bachelor's degree from university. Once you graduate and enter the workforce, you will have income and there are many ways to spend that money including paying off your student loan. If the student loan accrues a 6% annual interest rate, you would have to pay $250/month just to keep up with the interest and perhaps another $250 towards the principle for a total of $500/month. You will get into a routine of paying this monthly expense for about 8 years until it's fully paid off. Suddenly after 8 years, you no longer "have" to pay this $500/month. This money is now yours to spend however you wish. Not paying $500/month on something you have to is equivalent in making an additional $500/month in income. This brings me back to the point I wanted to illustrate earlier: **The money you don't pay is the money you make**.

Let's go through another simple example similar to the one from earlier involving the stock market. Imagine you have about $1000 in spendings on your credit card and the payment is due at the end of this month. A typical credit card has an interest rate of about 20% per year and you will need to pay that interest for any balance amount carried over to the next month or billing cycle. After getting your last paycheck of the month and making all of your purchases and paying all of your bills, you have $1000 left in cash. It's now time to decide how to spend this money.

Option 1: you can invest this $1000 in the stock market and as we talked about this previously, you can expect to get about a ~10% return on your money after 1 year. It is assumed after a year from now, you will have an additional $100 from the investment you just made. Neglecting all the minor details and the compounding effect, with a 20% interest rate, your new credit card balance is now $1200. So you just made $100 in profits from the stock market but you accrued a debt for the amount of $200 bringing your networth to -$100 after a year.

Option 2: instead of spending your $1000 in the stock market, you choose to pay your credit card balance immediately so that you are not accumulating any interest. At the end of one year, you have no gain from the stock market but you also have no debt from the interest accrued bringing your net total to $0.

Ask yourself, which is the better and more logical option? Sounds pretty obvious? You would be surprised.

Also, if you are one of those individuals who tend to carry credit card balance from month to month, definitely consider getting a card that has a much lower interest rate than 20%. They do exist! And they will save you a lot of money over time on interest costs.

CHAPTER 3: EMERGENCY FUND

I can not begin to stress the importance of having an emergency fund. It amazes me to see how some people spend so much money on things they don't need when they don't have an emergency fund. What is an emergency fund? How much should I allocate to this fund? And why would I even need an emergency fund to begin with? If you don't currently have an emergency fund and you are not asking yourself these questions, you seriously need to start.

No matter how well you think you can plan your life and manage your money and spendings, unexpected things do happen which most of the time are out of your control. But one thing you can do is to be prepared to handle it if the situation was ever to present itself.

Emergency fund is simply a saved up amount of cash that you don't touch under any circumstance; unless it is a true emergency.

What if you get laid off from your job due to some unfortunate event? If you have a working partner who can support you during these times, great. But not everyone has this luxury so being prepared is very critical. During unemployment, you still need to pay rent. You still need to buy groceries and food. You still need to pay your bills. You need to buy the day to day essentials for the next little while until you find your next job or your unemployment pay kicks in(or offset the difference if that is not enough). This is where having an emergency fund will pay off and spare you from the stress and pressure.

As mentioned earlier there are many unexpected events that arise in life. Your brand new car might break down and you might need to replace a very expensive part which you did not anticipate. You owe more income tax to the government than had initially anticipated. You might get a big medical bill for some accident or your fridge breaks down all of the sudden. Regardless of the reason, it is imperative to have an emergency fund to cover those large and unexpected expenses that get thrown your way. It provides a nice buffer and prevents you from resorting to credit cards which bring on more debt due to the nature of their high interest rates.

Typically the rule of thumb is you need at least about 3 months worth of your regular living expenses. But to be on the safe side, I'd recommend saving 6 months worth of expenses. Try and contribute regularly and consistently to build this fund as soon as you can. Don't consider investing your money in other places until this fund has been built. If your employer deposits the money into your checking account, transfer a reasonable amount to your savings account immediately. If your bank has the auto transfer or auto-save feature, set it up and let it run on auto-pilot.

I recommend building and leaving your emergency fund in a high yield savings account. This way your principal is not at any risk and fully insured(depending on your bank and amount). Your money is also not locked in so you can use it anytime. A savings account yielding around 2% interest per year is the perfect home for your emergency fund. You earn a little bit of cash through interest over time or at least your money does not lose its value to inflation.

Once you reach your goal and fully build the fund, it's always a good idea to continue on saving the extra cash at hand in a different savings account. This will allow you to plan and get organized for other financial goals such as taking a nice vacation or saving for a downpayment of a car or a house.

Having an emergency fund and building that cash reserve can help you weather most unexpected financial storms that may come your way.

CHAPTER 4: INVESTING IN THE STOCK MARKET

At first, the thought of investing in the stock market can be quite overwhelming; especially if you have no prior experience. But believe me, it's easy and anyone can do it. There are many different ways and approaches you can take to invest your hard earned cash into the stock market and profit from it. However, there are also a certain level of risks associated when investing in the stock market which could lead to potential capital losses. Thus, it is very important to be able to manage your risks. Again, as an investor, one of the hardest things you will have to do is to manage your risks. We will cover some of the key methods you can leverage to accomplish this throughout the chapter.

There are two popular ways of investing in the stock market:
1. Investing through individual companies that are trading publicly on a stock exchange
2. Investing in a collection of companies through a fund

The first method will require a lot of time and effort on your part. You need to be able to allocate a lot of time researching the company of your interest. You will need to go through their financial reports every quarter to keep track of their revenue, operating costs, debt, and so on. You will also need to be able to read and interpret their 10-K and 10-Q reports along with their MD&A document. You will then need to analyze the company's future growth using their business model, moat, sales, and EPS growth.

If you are anyone like me with a full time job and a lot less free time on your hands, investing through a fund might be the perfect solution. There are a lot of different types of funds out there created for different investor groups. One of the most popular types of funds is called an index fund. Index fund is a fund that mirrors a particular index. In simple terms, an index consists of a collection of companies selected by a committee based on different criterias and metrics. For example, the S&P 500 is an index that tracks the largest 500 companies in the United States. Nasdaq 100 is an index that tracks the 100 [1] largest and actively traded non-financial companies on the Nasdaq Stock Exchange that covers sectors such as technology, healthcare, and retail. S&P/TSX is an index that tracks the companies that trade on Canada's Toronto Stock Exchange (TSX). So to recap, an index includes a collection of publicly traded companies with each company having a specific weight (% allocation) in that particular index.

Top 10 Holdings (25.78% of Total Assets)

Name	Symbol	% Assets
Microsoft Corp	MSFT	5.52%
Apple Inc	AAPL	5.24%
Amazon.com Inc	AMZN	4.01%
Facebook Inc A	FB	2.14%
Alphabet Inc A	GOOGL	1.69%
Alphabet Inc Class C	GOOG	1.69%
Johnson & Johnson	JNJ	1.54%
Berkshire Hathaway Inc Class B	BRK.B	1.43%
Visa Inc Class A	V	1.32%
JPMorgan Chase & Co	JPM	1.20%

[2]

Figure 1: Top 10 holdings of the S&P 500 index by asset allocation

Figure 1 above shows the top 10 companies held in the S&P 500 index by % allocation. These allocations and the weight in the index can change at any time based on different criterias such as performance, revenue, and growth.

Figure 2 below outlines the performance of the same index. As can be seen, the index has an average return of approx. 10% per year since inception.

	As Of	1 Month	QTD	YTD	1 Year	3 Year	5 Year	10 Year	Since Inception Jan 22 1993
Fund Before Tax									
NAV	May 31 2020	4.74%	18.14%	-5.02%	12.65%	10.07%	9.72%	13.02%	9.39%
Market Value	May 31 2020	4.74%	18.02%	-5.05%	12.58%	10.05%	9.71%	13.01%	9.39%
S&P 500 Index	May 31 2020	4.76%	18.19%	-4.97%	12.84%	10.23%	9.86%	13.15%	9.52%

[3]

Figure 2: Cumulative performance of the S&P 500 index

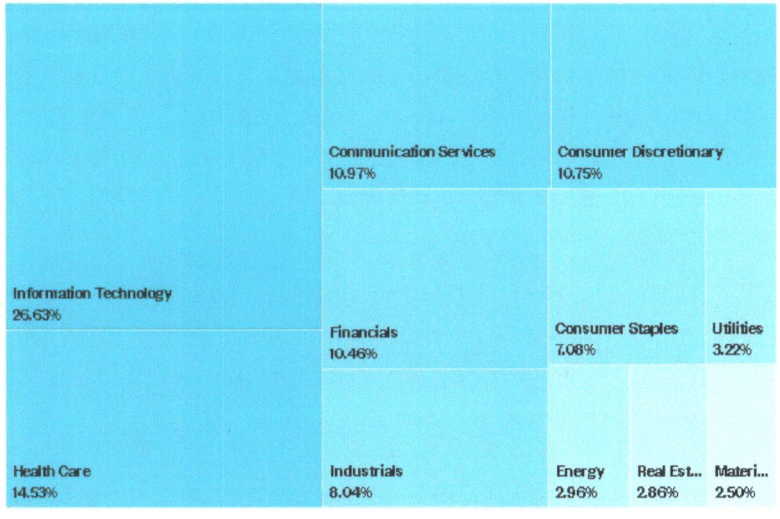

[4]

Figure 3: Sector allocation and breakdown of the S&P 500 index as of June 11, 2020

Figure 3 above illustrates the sector allocation and break down of the index. Understanding the sector allocation is very important as it helps us identify how diverse a specific index is.

Now that you have a good understanding of what an index is, let's talk about how you can invest in a particular index and what are some of the things you can do to make better, more educated decisions to help your overall success.

If you don't have the time nor the interest in picking individual stocks and you're seeking long-term growth, index funds are one of the best options out there at the moment. There are two very popular methods of investing in an index fund:
1. Mutual Funds
2. Exchange Traded Funds (ETFs)

Mutual funds are usually actively managed by a fund manager to reach a certain goal or follow a specific strategy and hence have higher management fees which are passed along to the investors. Management expense ratios (MER) typically run somewhere between 1%-3% depending on the provider and the type of fund.

ETFs are funds that follow a specific market or index and don't require active management which results in a much lower management fee. Management fees(MER) for ETF funds following a specific index can run between 0.05%-0.75%.

High management fees can eat into your investment's capital gain and growth especially on a 10-30 year time horizon. So you should try and avoid them if you can.

Since ETFs trade on the stock exchange, you would have to place a trade to buy more funds or sell your funds just like a regular stock. Keep in mind that there are always commission fees associated with buying and selling on an exchange.

In general, mutual funds and ETFs are similar in nature but they do have some differences. With mutual funds, you don't have to worry about managing or rebalancing your portfolio from time to time in exchange for paying the higher management fee. Also, in order to sell or buy more funds, you don't have to pay any commission fees. Another advantage of mutual funds is that you could set up pre-authorized transactions so that the money gets added from your bank account to your funds automatically on a timed interval(e.g. Once a month). This way you can stay hands off and your investment will be on auto-pilot. Note that sometimes mutual funds require minimum investment amounts and have this restriction in place. But those numbers are typically not that high. In addition, with mutual funds, you are able to buy partial shares or fractional units of a specific fund.

When investing via ETFs, you would have to be comfortable buying and selling on the stock exchange. As mentioned earlier, most brokerages will charge you commission fees when buying or selling on the stock exchange. Also with ETFs, you might need to rebalance your portfolio from time to time (once or twice a year) but since you manage this yourself, they come with a very low MER cost. Furthermore, at the time of this book's publication, you are not able to set up pre-authorized transactions to automate your investing with ETFs.

ETFs work great for passive, DIY investors and long term strategies so we will focus on those for the remainder of this chapter.

In order to invest in an index fund, you will first need to open a direct investing account with a brokerage. There are a lot of different investing account types out there with various different tax rules depending on where you live and your investing goals(short-term, growth, retirement).

Most brokerages nowadays have financial advisors to help you choose the right account type and investment strategy. So be sure to speak to one if you need help choosing the right account type for you. In addition, when choosing a brokerage for your investing needs, be sure to consider one that is well known and one that is properly insured. TD, Fidelity, and Charles Schwab are some of the popular ones in the United States.

Once you have opened your account with the broker of your choice, you are now ready to begin your investing journey by placing trades(buy/sell orders). Also, when purchasing ETFs, be sure to go with a well known provider. Vanguard and Blackrock(iShares) are some of the biggest ETF providers across US and Canada and a popular choice amongst the investing community. Before starting to buy ETFs, be sure to have an investing strategy and plan in place. The ETFs you buy will shape your long term portfolio and will play an important role in your future success. We will now examine some common model portfolios out there used by the majority of long term investors.

Even though there are currently over 3000+ companies in the United States, The S&P 500 index is a good indicator of how well the overall US stock market performed in a given year. This makes the S&P 500 ETF a good choice for your portfolio as:
- It is well diversified across large cap companies in different sectors
- You are not investing in a single stock(safety in numbers)
- You don't need to research the individual companies

If the S&P 500 index goes up 10% in a year, the value of your ETF fund will also go up by 10%. If the S&P 500 index goes down 5%, then the market value of your ETF will go down by 5%. Although the future performance of any index is unknown at the present time, it is pretty clear the overall stock market tends to go up over the long term from historical data and charts. This makes the S&P 500 ETF an ideal choice for long term investors. SPY and VOO are a couple of examples of the S&P 500 ETFs both trading on the NYSEArca exchange. As a side, you can always use your brokerage or free apps and websites such as Yahoo Finance to search for these ticker symbols and dig up more information. Alternatively, you can research a specific ETF on their provider's official website. SPY is provided by State Street Global Advisors. VOO is provided by Vanguard.

If you are a more conservative investor and would like to reduce risk or volatility in your portfolio, you can choose to invest in the Total US Market ETF instead. It's a low cost way of owning the entire US stock market in your portfolio. It is also more diversified than the S&P 500 as not only it covers the large cap stocks, but it also covers midcap and small-cap stocks as well. ITOT is an example of a Total US Stock Market ETF provided by iShares. VTI is another ETF provided by Vanguard that covers the same index.

If you would like to add further diversification to your portfolio, you may look into purchasing an ETF that follows the MSCI EAFE Index. The MSCI EAFE Index captures the equity performance of the market across developed countries excluding the U.S. and Canada. EFA is one ETF you can purchase that mirrors this index.

If you would like to diversify even more, you could consider adding the Emerging Market index to your equity portfolio to capture more of the global landscape. VWO is an example ETF provided by Vanguard for this index.

Once you have determined which ETFs you would like to use to build your portfolio along with their respective asset allocation, it's time to de-risk your portfolio by introducing bonds. Bonds are conservative fixed-income investments which introduce stability to an all-equity portfolio. Bonds usually pay a dividend of 2%-3% annually which provide a steady source of income and help your investment beat inflation at the least.

Occasionally(but not always) when the stock market crashes and the economy enters a recession due to loss of consumer spending, interest rates are lowered which drives the bond prices up. In this scenario, if you need to free up cash for whatever reason, you are selling your bonds at a profit or you could sell your bonds to buy more equities to dollar cost average while the prices remain low.

So now the question becomes how much of my portfolio should I hold in equities and how much in bonds? The answer depends on your risk tolerance and investing time horizon.

If you are young and have about 30-40 years until retirement, it is suggested that you take more of an aggressive approach(more equities and less bonds) and switch to a more conservative portfolio as you are getting closer to retirement(more bonds and less equities).

The figure below represents 5 asset allocation model portfolios you can consider:

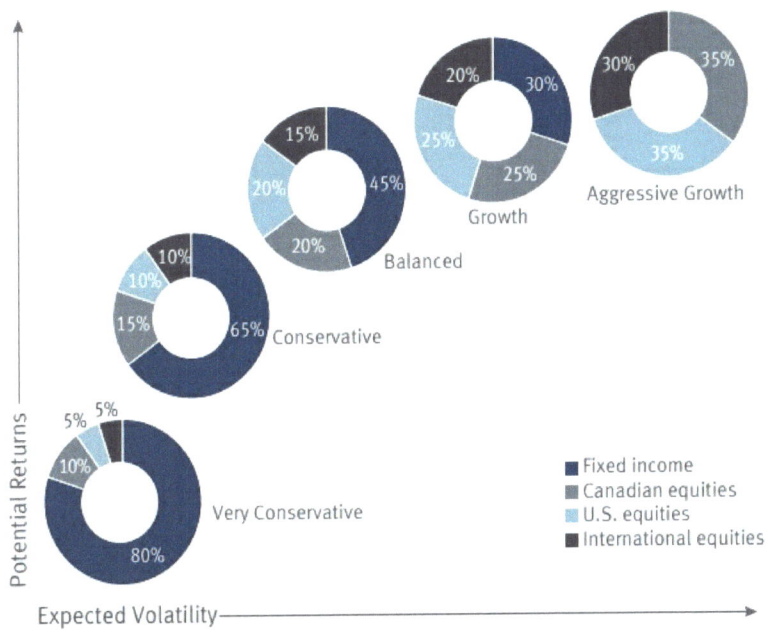

Figure 4: Asset Allocation Model Portfolios by RBC Global Asset Management

Figure 5 below shows the asset allocation breakdown and historical returns for a sample growth portfolio.

Figure 5(a): Asset type mix for a sample growth portfolio

Figure 5(b): Annual performance of a sample growth portfolio

By now you should have a pretty good understanding of what index funds are and how to build a portfolio using mutual funds or ETFs.

Whether you choose to go with Mutual Funds or ETFs, pick one that has a low MER and follows a particular index; especially one that you understand. Choose a broker that is

well known and properly insured and also allows you to buy ETFs commission free. There are some out there!
Once you start, stick with your plan and ignore all the noise. Seek advice once in a while from a financial advisor and try to rebalance your portfolio once or twice a year to maintain your target asset allocation.

Concept of rebalancing is quite simple and easy to grasp. Markets typically fluctuate at different rates during different times. For example, given you have a growth portfolio, you may start the year with the perfect 80/20 asset allocation mix. However, by the end of the same year that may have changed to 90/10 due to market performance. The act of rebalancing is to sell a portion of the equity assets in your portfolio and use that same money to buy into more bonds to bring back the asset allocation to 80/20 again.

Rebalancing is quite important as it helps ensure your portfolio is not over exposed to unnecessary risks. It also helps lower the risk to a level that is more desirable and tolerable by you, the investor.

One last important note I would like to highlight is the dividend aspect associated with both the equity and bond portion of the portfolio. Dividend is interest paid out to shareholders in the form of cash. Although at first glance it might seem attractive to take that cash and spend it all(it is free money after all), it is highly recommended to invest that cash back into the portfolio to help it grow faster. This is what is referred to as the compound effect. Imagine you are trying to push a snowball uphill. It is very difficult at the start as you have to fight your way through a steep slope and the snowball grows larger in size but at a very slow rate. When you reach the peak and start to go downhill, things start to get easier. The snowball starts to pick up momentum and speed and as it is rolling down, it grows bigger at a much faster rate than it did initially You can achieve the same effect with your investments and portfolio if you reinvest the dividends back on top of your periodic contribution.

If you have a long time horizon and don't need that cash, think about reinvesting that back into your portfolio to help you reach your goals faster. Most stocks and ETFs allow you to enroll in the dividend reinvestment plan(DRIP).

DRIP allows you to reinvest your cash from your dividend payout. It is a great option to have enabled on your account because it automatically reinvests that cash back to purchase additional shares of that specific ETF or stock without charging you any commission fees throughout the process.

CHAPTER 5: STREAMS OF INCOME

Whether you want to reach your financial, retirement, and investing goals early or if you just need some extra cash for your vacations, increasing your streams of income is one of the best possible solutions; especially if you are someone like me with an average salary. We'll cover a few simple methods you can try in this chapter which may seem pretty obvious at first. But believe me when I say that it'll have a huge impact on your life.

Generating passive income is one of many good options to consider if you want to increase your financial net worth more rapidly. I recommend this method because it's easier to start with in comparison to other ways we will cover shortly. The idea behind passive income is that you do something once and you will continuously get paid for it thereafter. It's easy to get started with passive income because you will require either of the following two things: money or time. But just know that your success does depend upon a lot of hard work and dedication at the early stages of your venture. There are different avenues of creating passive income but investing in a dividend stock is a good simple one. Generally, publicly-traded companies choose to spend their earnings in two ways:

1. Put the earnings and revenue made back into the business to help it grow
   - This results in a faster stock price appreciation over time(growth)
2. Pay out a portion of their earnings to the shareholders to reward them for investing in the company
   - This creates a steady source of income for shareholders if the company stays healthy and continues to make profit in the future (dividend)

Dividend investing has become very popular recently as everyone loves a steady source of income. However, this will require you to have initial money to invest. In addition, you will need to spend your time researching good dividend companies with decent dividend yields. AT&T Inc.(ticker:T), Verizon Communications Inc.(ticker:VZ), and Philip Morris International Inc.(ticker:PM) are a few examples of dividend paying companies. You can start by looking at some that are within the S&P 500 Index and go from there. Also, it is always good to consider the track record for a company's dividend:

- How long have they been paying dividends to their shareholders?
- Have they increased their dividend rate over time?
- How did the share price appreciate over time?
  - You don't want to invest in a company that pays out all of their earnings as dividends preventing it from further growth

If you are not comfortable investing in individual dividend stocks, you can take the ETF route! There are ETF funds out there that track a dividend index that could hold roughly about 50-80 companies for example. VYM is an example of a dividend ETF provided by Vanguard. SPYD is another good example of a high yield dividend paying ETF.

Another option is to invest in real estate investment trusts (REITs). These are companies that usually own real estate properties or invest in the real estate sector. If you're interested in real estate and can't own a property directly(or just don't want to), REITs are a great alternative. Most REITs have a high dividend yield. In addition, real estate in general, is a good long-term investment. Do your research to make sure you find a good high quality REIT or fund of REITs before investing.

If you are not comfortable investing via dividend stocks or equities in general due to their risk or possible major fluctuations, bonds would make for a great choice due to the nature of their low volatility. Bonds typically don't fluctuate that often and some usually yield a nice dividend rate of 2%-3%. Hence this makes investing in a bond fund or ETF a good and reliable source of passive income. One example is the iShares U.S. Aggregate Bond ETF(ticker: AGG on NYSEArca) which yields around 2.46%[8] annual dividend.

Another good source of passive income is simply keeping your cash in a high yield savings account. Some savings accounts yield between 0.5% to 3% of interest which may not seem like a big gain at first. But would you rather make 2% interest on your principal or 0% if you were to hold the same amount of cash in a chequing account?

In addition, unlike dividend stocks or bonds, your principal amount is always guaranteed and at no risk. As mentioned previously, always try to understand how the bank is insuring your money and upto what amount for any given account by reading the details and all the fine prints.

There are other sources of income streams that do not involve investing money, but rather your time. If you are truly good at something like statistics, science, or programming and you have a passion for teaching, consider bundling your skill sets and experience into a course. This course can then be distributed on various online platforms. Not only will it provide a nice source of income, but you are also helping someone out there learn something new quickly and in a cost effective manner. Depending on the platform, you could get paid a certain % of each purchase or simply by the number of minutes watched. There are many many platforms out there and some allow you to get started without any additional costs to becoming a teacher. Some examples are Pluralsight, Linked-In learning or you can simply host and market your own course on teachable.com.

It's always important to do a bit of research to understand the market demand and existing courses out there to avoid the saturated segments by finding the right niche to become more successful and profitable.

Creating content on YouTube is yet another way to increase your sources of income. If you are comfortable with public speaking and have some basic video editing skills, you will be able to create a YouTube channel and monetize your videos on the platform. In order to have the ability to enable monetization, you will require a minimum number of subscribers and minutes watched each month which means you have to be very careful and selective in the videos you produce. It's important to always create meaningful educational content so that people can take away something new by watching your videos. Once you have enough subscribers, you can begin to get your videos sponsored or choose to display ads to increase your revenue. Also, when you are well established after sometime, you can use your YouTube channel as a means of distribution for other products such as affiliate marketing or selling your own merchandise which are both quite popular these days.

There are other simple ways of increasing your source of income. If you are good at math, consider tutoring someone who is not. If you are good at playing the piano, consider teaching someone who is passionate about music and learning instruments. If you have something sitting at home that you don't need, consider selling it on a platform such as eBay or Craigslist. This way you make some money and you have more living space at home. These side hustles are easy and won't take more than a few hours per week. And the best part; you are in charge of your own schedule and pace.

If you are someone who does have the initial seed money or capital, real estate investing could be a good choice. Just like with the stock market, you can have a real estate portfolio consisting of multiple properties. Rental property income is a good method of increasing your overall cash flow especially if the property was purchased in full and does not require a mortgage; reducing risk towards your other investments. Not all properties have to be purchased brand new. If you are looking to purchase a property for rental income, consider a place that is not too old but can be renovated with a bit of money and does not have a ridiculous maintenance/association fee.

Finding a good location with easy access to metro or transit and close to schools or shopping malls is the key for being able to rent out your property with ease.

When planning the purchase of a property for rental income, not everything in your wishlist will perfectly align. Be sure to settle on what things are important to you so that when the opportunity does arise, you can execute your plan quickly.

Furthermore, if your properties have gained a significant amount of appreciation over a short period of time, you can always consider selling the property and investing the money back into properties that are cheaper and currently undervalued.

CHAPTER 6: CASH IS TRASH

You might have heard the expression "cash is trash" from financial advisors or investment fund managers. The meaning? Exactly like as it sounds. Seating on a certain amount of cash is always a good idea as we discussed in the emergency fund chapter. You will always need cash at hand to deal with unforeseen and unanticipated circumstances. However, seating on a lot of cash is never a good idea. Why? Just like a car, cash loses its value over time.

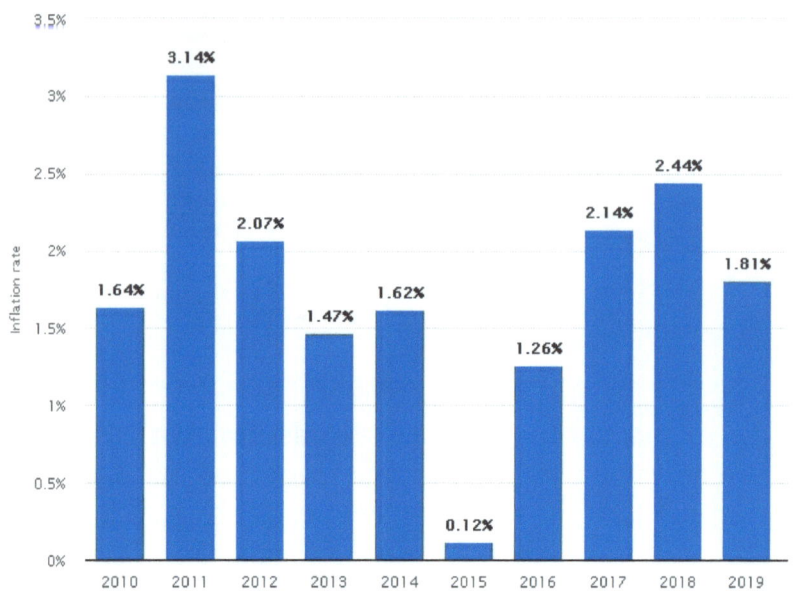

[9]

Figure 6: Annual inflation rate in the United States from 2010 to 2019

Figure 6 above shows that the average inflation rate in the United States is roughly around 2% per year. This means that if you are sitting on just cash, you are losing 2% of your wealth. This is very important to understand and wrap your head around. Imagine this year you have about $1000 in cash which you can use to make purchases and buy select goods. Next year, due to inflation and increased cost of living, the same $1000 will buy you less goods compared to previous year, decreasing your overall buying power.

We typically go through a recession approximately once every decade or so and the severity of the recession depends on many factors. When the economy enters into a recession, the unemployment rates rise which means the consumer spending will go down. This creates a big problem as the majority of GDP(gross domestic product) comes from consumer spending. At this stage, the governments usually need to step in and intervene with various methods to help prevent the economy from collapsing. One way is to print more money which means "more cash". Another way is to lower interest rates. This means consumers can easily borrow money without having to pay hefty interest fees which again means "more cash". This helps drive up the consumer spending and stimulate the economy during a recession.

One interesting thing to note is that during a recession, the inflation rate is usually lower than the average rate but spikes up by a factor of multiple folds roughly about a year after the recession's end. This can be seen in Figure 6 below which shows Canada's inflation rate from 1984 to 2021 with attention to the early 1990's and the 2009 housing crisis.[10]

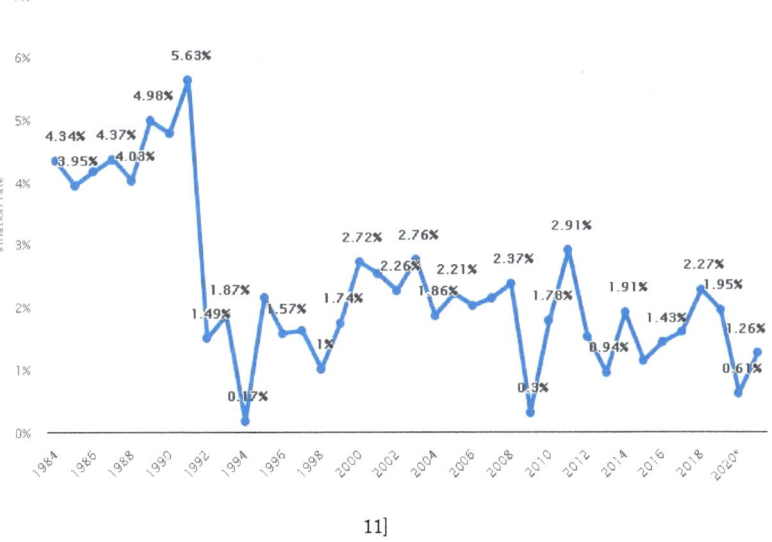

11]

Figure 6: Canada's inflation rate from 1984 to 2021

It is always good to have a certain amount of cash set aside for things that you don't anticipate in life. But having too much money in a form of cash is generally not a good idea. You should always invest your cash so that it is working for you by either creating more wealth or making you happy in different areas of life which we covered throughout this book.

Nevertheless, depending on your situation and risk tolerance, if you must hold on to cash, consider a high yield savings account. If you can find one with an interest rate of about 2%, you are breaking even with the annual inflation. Hence the value of your money remains the same year to year. There are also other similar options available worth considering depending on your appetite. Money Market(investing in short-term debt) is one option. There are different ways of investing in the money market.

One way is through money market funds which can be purchased through different banks or brokers. These funds don't typically change in price and they pay interest. Another way is to purchase short-term certificate of deposits(CDs). CDs are products that can be purchased from a bank and typically pay a nice premium interest rate. In exchange for that interest, you agree to leave your money locked in for a predetermined period of time. This is a good option if you know you won't need the money for the next little while.

Municipal Notes are another vehicle that can be used to invest in the money market. They are offered by the local or state governments and typically mature in a year's time. This is favoured amongst some investors as it is considered a fixed-income asset and also includes some tax advantages. At the maturity date, you will receive your principle along with the interest that occurred during that period.

Purchasing U.S. Treasury Bills (T-Bill) is another way of investing in the money market. T-Bills are short-term debt backed by the U.S. Treasury departments and usually mature in about a year or less. The longer the maturity date, the higher the interest that will be paid out to the investor.

Treasury Inflation-Protected Security (TIPS) is yet another option you can consider to help protect your buying power against inflation. With TIPS, your principal amount is protected and you will never receive less than your initial investment's dollar amount. As the inflation rises, so does the value of your investment and you also receive interest payment which may vary depending on the gain on your principle.

The options you have available may vary depending on where you live. For example, if you live in Canada, you have access to Guaranteed Investment Certificates(GICs) through your bank. Just like CDs, you can earn interest on your money by agreeing to leave it untouched for a preset period of time. The longer the maturity date, the more interest you will gain. You may also purchase GICs from third party banks via investment brokers which means you're not limited just to your own bank.

Market Growth GICs is a variation that some people including myself may favour over traditional GICs. This type of GIC provides a minimum interest rate to investors but has a cap higher than your average traditional GICs. These GICs are linked to the performance of the stock market. For instance, let's say the minimum interest rate is 1% and the cap is 12%. So if the stock market does not perform very well, you still get back your principal plus the minimum interest rate(1%) at maturity. But if the stock market performs well, you will get back your principal plus upto 12% of interest on your initial principle which is a considerable amount when compared with other GICs.

One example is the TD Canadian Banking and Utilities GIC which is offering upto 12% with the maturity date of 3 years.[12]

If you choose to withdraw early(before the maturity date) you may be subject to losing the interest you earned or other fees and penalties. So be sure to understand how long you are able to keep your money locked-in for before considering this option.

CHAPTER 7: DIVERSIFICATION

Diversification is a key component of investing in all areas of your life. Diversification helps you protect yourself and your other investments by reducing exposure to different types of risks. Minimizing risk can help you achieve your goals quicker regardless of what they may be. We have touched on diversification in different chapters throughout this book covering multiple examples.

When you have multiple sources of income, you are protecting yourself against unfortunate events that might affect one(or more) of those sources. If you lose your full-time job or a primary source of income due to some unforeseen circumstance, you will still need to pay your rent or mortgage and other living expenses. Having multiple sources of income can help provide a nice buffer and relieve that financial stress temporarily, until you are able to find another job. Or you could simply use the income from your other sources to pay for unexpected expenses such as unplanned vacations or medical bills. Or the income could simply accumulate into a larger egg nest for future plans and help you reach financial freedom sooner than planned. This is the power of diversification.

When investing in the stock market, it is extremely important to consider diversification. When you are investing in a basket or collection of well researched blue-chip companies, if one was to go bankrupt due to whatever reason, you are reducing your risk of losing all of your money. If you are investing in companies across different sectors, you are reducing your portfolio from high volatility because not all sectors perform the same during the same time period. If you are investing in companies across multiple countries in different continents, you are reducing your risk and exposure to possible economic recessions or financial crises. Your equity portfolio would still hold strong and wouldn't drop as much compared to a portfolio that has an exposure to just one country. This is what I call a multi-layer diversification(backup for your backup). This might reduce your gains by a few percentage annually but it will also help reduce your risk dramatically and prevent you from destroying your investment accounts. Believe me when I say; you will sleep easier at night. This is a power of diversification.

In addition, if you have a portfolio that has a certain amount allocated to fixed-income assets, not only are you reducing your risk to the stock market volatility, but you are also benefiting from that 1%-3% steady source of income provided by the interest from those assets. The right asset allocation is the key when focusing on long-term performance and short-term volatility.

This is why it is so important to talk to a financial advisor and also do your research to create a plan before putting your investment portfolio together. Diversification should be one of the key factors on top of your list when creating a portfolio. This is one of the hardest and most challenging parts of investing. But, once you have a proper plan, the rest becomes a walk in the park. You just simply execute your plan and stick with it. The primary goal of diversification is not to maximize your capital gains but to reduce volatility in your portfolio, especially as you get closer to retirement or other financial goals.

The concept of diversification does not always just tie into the financial markets or investment portfolios. There are many things you can do to diversity your life and your everyday routines which could help you become happier as an individual.

Exploring new ideas is one effective way. Everyone has ideas that they constantly think about so why not try a couple? Maybe you want to start your own business, or you want to try a new sport, or maybe you want to try a new process that could help you or others become more effective at work. Why not give your ideas a try?

Some people are afraid of trying new things and maybe for a good reason. However, it is very important to try and get out of your comfort zone by breaking out of your daily routines and giving new things a try for several reasons. First, you might actually enjoy the new thing you are exploring. This could lead to diversification of your repeated daily routines. Second, you will most likely learn something new or meet someone new and like-minded as part of the process.

Meeting new people is another interesting way to diversify in life. Meeting new people exposes you to new characteristics, ideas, and a pool of experiences that you could have never thought possible. These will create a great learning experience for you and can help develop the skills necessary to devise plans or solutions if you were to come across similar problems or obstacles in your path of life. Helpful knowledge from others, can save you the time and pain of having to go through that yourself by being ready if the situation was to present itself. Also, sometimes by meeting new people, you will learn some of the things that you should not do in life.

These are invaluable lessons that you will not learn in school but essential to guide you down a happy and cheerful life. **This is the power of diversification.**

CHAPTER 8: STAY FOCUSED

Nothing comes easy in life (for most of us anyways) so it is imperative to stay focused if you want to become successful and achieve your goals. If you have to learn something new to make advancements in your career, you have to make sacrifices. You have to put in the extra time and effort unlike others. Do you think it's easy going to class at night after a long hard day at work? Do you think it's easy sacrificing your weekends taking an online course while all of your friends are out clubbing? Believe me, it's not. Been there done that.

If you want to succeed, you have to stay focused and ignore distractions that are surrounding you. You have to push through the grind and put in the extra time. But don't lose track of the things or the people who are essential to your happiness. Watching 1 hour of TV might be something that makes you happy but it's definitely something you can give up for the time being until you reach your goals.

If you are in the process of paying down debt, focus your purchasing power on the things you absolutely need. Skip out on the things you don't need. If you have a ton of credit card debt for example, there is no need for you to have a $5 cup of coffee every day of the week. Buy in bulk, make it yourself and focus the savings towards your debt. Your lifestyle won't change if you don't buy a brand new pair of clothes in the next couple of months. But focusing those savings towards your debt could have a significant impact on your lifestyle later down the road. Remember, this is just temporary. Once you reach your goals and debt free, you can go back to your daily routines. But hopefully not back to the habits that got you in that debt in the first place.

If your goal is to own a property or a car for example, focus on saving up for that. Don't invest your money in anything risky knowing that you will need it soon for a downpayment. If your goal is to build an emergency fund, focus on building a cash pile and don't invest it in the stock market until you reach your goal. Save most of your income and don't buy the things that you don't need until your emergency fund has reached its cap. If you want to go on vacation, save for it ahead of time and just focus your money on that.

When you want to invest in the stock market, focus on your plan and strategy first. Try and understand why you are investing and what are your short-term and long-term plans. You should focus on having a plan for various situations such as an economic recession or market correction where prices could pull back significantly. You should never invest the money that you know you will need within the next 12 months. And that's why we have an emergency fund! In case you do make that mistake.
If your portfolio takes a hit, don't panic and try to win back that loss through other means. Stay focused and keep your consistency. Continue contributing as per your plan on regular intervals to average down during market down-

trends. In fact, market down trends create one of the best opportunities to build up a bigger position and grow your portfolio which helps accelerate your original plan. Do not invest in things that you don't understand. And do not invest in something solely from the fear of missing out. Cryptocurrency surge in 2017 is the perfect example.

Always focus on analyzing risks and plan on reducing them to tilt the odds in your favour, no matter what you plan. Once you start, stay consistent and filter out all the noise from your surroundings that cause unnecessary distractions or help deviate from your original goal. Stay strong and motivated even if you don't see results to start with. Be flexible and open minded so that you could change your plans to better suit your needs without punishing yourself if mistakes are made. Be passionate about your goals in life and stay driven. Drive and determinations are the key to success.

FINAL WORDS

In order to become successful in life, you have to work hard. You have to recognize and evaluate your strengths and weaknesses. You have to ask for feedback and accept criticism. You need the ability to formulate a plan and execute without getting distracted. What you learn about yourself during the process will be invaluable.

Understand what things make you happy consciously. If you are happy but don't know why, you won't be able to maintain it. If you are unhappy and don't know why, you will remain unhappy. If you want financial freedom, you need to educate yourself and start early. Find a balance between your spendings and don't let debt take control of your life.

Don't invest in things that you don't understand. Don't invest in stocks that are hot, thinking you will double or triple your money in a short period of time. Don't invest in them from the fear of missing out. Success doesn't come overnight. Success comes from long periods of hard work and dedication. Apply yourself and remain patient.

Try and stay disciplined and focus on the big picture. Think long term. Ignore all the noise around you and stick with executing your plan. Ask for help or revise if you are not seeing results. There is no shame in making mistakes. You just have to learn from them and try not to make the same mistake twice. Manage your risks properly and have a plan to cover yourself in cases of unforeseen events. Life is dynamic so you should be too. Work hard and play hard. Always try and enjoy life. After all, we only live once so choose to be happy.

Thank you for taking the time to read this book. If you have enjoyed reading this book or if you have learned something new and valuable, I would appreciate an honest feedback on Amazon where this book is currently published. I would also greatly appreciate you recommending this book to anyone who you think would benefit from the content.

GLOSSARY

10-K:

10k is a report document that every publicly traded company needs to file with the security stock exchange (SEC) every year highlighting the company's financial performance.

10-Q:
Similar to a 10-K report, 10-Q is a report representing a publicly traded company's financials that needs to be filed every quarter with the SEC.

A

APR: Annual Percentage Rate represents the annual interest amount on the borrowed amount.

C

Compounding effect: compounding effect is the increasing value of your investment due to an increase on both your principle and ongoing accumulated interest over a time period.

D

DIY: Do It Yourself
DRIP: Dividend Reinvestment Plan

E

EPS: EPS is a number that is calculated from dividing the company's net profit by the number of outstanding shares. Higher EPS means you are getting more value from your investment.

G

GDP: Gross domestic product is a measure of a country's overall domestic production.

I

Inception: Inception is a creation date of a specific fund.

M

MD&A: Management discussion and analysis is a section of the company's financial report containing information about the financial performance and is presented by the management group.

Moat: Moat is a type of advantage a company has over others such as brand or patents.

N

NAV: Net asset value is a number that is calculated by subtracting the funds total assets from its total liabilities(such as debt)

S

S&P 500: S&P 500 is an index consisting of the largest 500 companies in the United States. It is often used as a benchmark to see how well the overall market is performing.

T

TIPS: Treasury Inflation-Protected is a treasury bond. Its value rises as the inflation goes up protecting investors from inflation and keeping their buying power the same. The bond also pays interest to investors.

---

[1] This is a rough number and subject to change at anytime without notice based on different criterias

[2] Taken from Yahoo Finance on June 12th, 2020

[3] Taken from State Street Global Advisors' website: https://www.ssga.com/

[4] Taken from State Street Global Advisors' website: https://www.ssga.com/

[5] Taken from https://www.rbcgam.com/

[6] Taken from RBC's Global Asset Management website https://www.rbcgam.com/

[7] Taken from RBC's Global Asset Management website https://www.rbcgam.com/

[8] Please note this rate is subject to change at any time

[9] Data taken from statista.com

[10] Please note the inflation rate for 2020 and 2021 is a projected rate at the time this book was written

[11] Data taken from statista.com

[12] As of June 28, 2020. This rate is subject to change at any time

www.ingramcontent.com/pod-product-compliance
Lightning Source LLC
Chambersburg PA
CBHW040240220526
45473CB00001B/311